World of Farming

Farm Animals

Nancy Dickmann

Heinemann Library
Chicago, Illinois

www.capstonepub.com
Visit our website to find out
more information about
Heinemann-Raintree books.

To order:

☎ Phone 800-747-4992

▣ Visit www.capstonepub.com
to browse our catalog and order online.

©2011 Heinemann Library
an imprint of Capstone Global Library, LLC
Chicago, Illinois

Edited by Siân Smith, Nancy Dickmann, and Rebecca Rissman
Designed by Joanna Hinton-Malivoire
Picture research by Mica Brancic
Production by Victoria Fitzgerald
Originated by Capstone Global Library Ltd
Printed and bound in the United States of America in
North Mankato, Minnesota.   072015   009127RP

17 16 15
10 9 8 7

Library of Congress Cataloging-in-Publication Data
Dickmann, Nancy.
  Farm animals / Nancy Dickmann.—1st ed.
     p. cm.—(World of farming)
  Includes bibliographical references and index.
  ISBN 978-1-4329-3934-2 (hc)—ISBN 978-1-4329-3941-0 (pb)
1. Domestic animals—Juvenile literature. 2. Livestock—Juvenile literature.
I. Title. II. Series: Dickmann, Nancy. World of farming.
  SF75.5.D53 2010
  636—dc22
                                        2009052336

Acknowledgements
We would like to thank the following for permission to reproduce
photographs: Photolibrary pp.**4** (F1 Online/Photo Thomas Gruener), **5**
(Robert Harding Travel/Robert Harding), **6** (age fotostock/Stuart Pearce),
7 (Fresh Food Images/Gerrit Buntrock), **8** (Westend61/Gerald Staufer),
9 (Flirt Collection/Julie Habel), **10** (Ableimages/julian winslow), **11**
(Juniors Bildarchiv), **12** (Oxford Scientific (OSF)/Colin Monteath), **13**
(Superstock/Superstock Inc), **14** (First Light Associated Photographers/Brian
Summers), **15** (All Canada Photos/Steve Ogle), **16** (Tips Italia/Sergio Tafner
Jorge), **17** (age fotostock/Leonardo Diaz Romero), **18** (Geoff Higgins),
19 (Juniors Bildarchiv), **20** (Moodboard RF), **21** (Index Stock Imagery/
Henry Horenstein), **22** (Fresh Food Images/Gerrit Buntrock), **23 top**, **23
middle** (age fotostock/Leonardo Diaz Romero), **23 bottom** (Superstock/
Superstock Inc).

Front cover photograph of spring lambs grazing in a field reproduced
with permission of iStockPhoto (locke_rd). Back cover photograph of a
border collie dog, working merino sheep reproduced with permission of
Photolibrary (Geoff Higgins).

The publisher would like to thank Dee Reid, Diana Bentley, and Nancy Harris
for their invaluable help with this book.

Contents

What Is a Farm?

A farm is a place where food
is grown.

Many animals live on a farm.

Animals on a Farm

Cows live on a farm.

Some cows give us milk.

Chickens live on a farm.

Some chickens lay eggs.

Pigs live on a farm.

Pigs love to roll around in the mud.

Sheep live on a farm.

wool

Sheep give us wool.

Some farms have ducks.

llama

Some farms have llamas.

Working Animals

Horses can help move cows.

Oxen can help pull plows.

Dogs can help move sheep.

Cats can help catch rats and mice.

Taking Care of Farm Animals

Farm animals need food and water.

Farm animals need a safe place to sleep.

Can You Remember?

Which animals give us milk?

Answer on page 24

Picture Glossary

 **oxen** cows or bulls that are trained to pull plows or do other farm jobs

 **plow** farm machine that breaks up the ground so that farmers can plant seeds

 **wool** hairy body covering on sheep. Wool can be made into clothes and blankets.

Index

Answer to quiz on page 22: Cows give us milk.

Note to Parents and Teachers

Before reading:
Ask the children if they have ever visited a farm. Do they know anyone who lives on a farm? Make a list together of all the farm animals they can think of. Ask them why they think these animals live on a farm.

After reading:
• Sing "Old MacDonald Had a Farm" together. Hold up pictures of each animal to prompt the children to make the correct animal noise.

• Talk to the children about page 17. Do they see cows pulling plows in their country? What is used instead? Ask them why they think cows and horses are used instead of machines in some countries.